TROJAN HORSES AND SECRET SPIES WHO BREAK INDIA

OR HOW 1% OF THE A̶I̶ ̶.̶.̶.̶.̶R̶O̶T̶E̶S̶T̶ANT CHURCH WITH THE HELP OF CHRISTIAN VATICAN CHURCH AND MULTI NATIONAL COMPANIES HIJACKED THE WHOLE OF AMERICA AND THE REST OF THE WORLD INCLUDING INDIA?

So, the 99% of the American people should wake up and help uphold "universal ethics" in the world!

Please visit my blog where I elaborated on the subject of this book. Here is its link:

https://panindiahindu.wordpress.com/

By CANAGARADJA Ganessane

1)Introduction: appetizer

2) Development: Main course: Putting myself in the body and mind of the 1% of the oligarchy of the US, I speak ...I develop the subject through their lens imagining what would have been their thinking which was behind their actions of breaking INIDA especially and the rest of the world. (22 FORMULAS THE ENEMIES OF INDIA APPLY IN THEIR HARD WORK OF BREAKING AND SUBVERTING INDIA

3) Conclusion: Dessert

I think the conclusion is simple: when dharma or universal ethics is not behind a word uttered or an action undertaken, then the result is the main content of this book itself where I describe the consequences of the absence of "dharma" in the mind of leaders of the world.

We, INDIANS, should collaborate with 99% of the silent masses of America to infuse "dharmic principle" in the heart of American governance and supplant the existing "greed and material based" thinking.

4) Appendix:

Caution: whenever I employ the generic term "west", understand it as this 1% of the oligarchy which forms a global club of world manipulators of the silent masses.

The APPETIZER / Introduction:

Why we can affirm without much exaggeration that Hinduism or "SANATANA DHARMA" is one of the best ways to lead a happy life on earth? First you should know that USA (1% of American population who are members of FORD or ROTHCHILD foundation club) manipulating the process of selecting and distributing this Nobel PRIZE ; as they are dualistic and monotheistic , their mindset functions on perceiving the other as different and not equal to them : The root cause of the Western suffering comes from the source of dualistic mindset or the binary way of thinking that India's "rishis" called "DVAITA" ; they think "the Red Indian " is so different (and perhaps the greed factor also contributed to their perception of the other as ready to be exploited) that they finished them off : this ultra-sensitivity to other's difference blinds their perception and makes them incapable of putting themselves in other's place. So, they almost completely eliminated them thereby committing the worst genocide whose perpetrators had never been punished: they also apply this phobia to their own people when their skin has a different colour and even among themselves when their neighbour is poor and not belonging to the same "new world order». In short, they function using the formula "they versus

5

us and inside their own community "me versus him"!

When they see that poor animal native to their colonised American soil, they perceived in that BISON one more life so different from their conception that they completely exterminated almost that animal population in America. They suffer from what I call "difference phobia" which is a by-product of monotheistic and Abrahamic mentality : poor guys whenever they see someone different , they try to evangelise him and "homogenise" him to their "cut-out format of racial, cultural standard" and if they cannot fit in , at least they make them mentally equivalent to them. Poor guys: Now, they are now taking forward aggressive globalisation scarifying their own middle-class people's jobs.

First of all, Americans have to abandon their job of "global POLICE" and treat India in par with any white nation. They discriminate INDIA and reserve always a special status to other western nations. All this comes from the "obsession of duality" which in turn provokes the incapacity to put oneself in other's place which is why Abrahamic religion is the source from where this magma of duality erupts, this in turn spoils all their way of thinking and adds karma to whatever action they do under the impulse of that adharmic way of thinking. From a cactus, we cannot expect a mango so also from this "duality" obsessed mind-set, we cannot expect "brotherhood" but only sectarian or selective brotherhood that is they are brothers within their race and community and country but never can they have the same feelings for another country's people. All these comes from the wrong mind-set. So, "O West, discard your Abrahamic dual insanity." Indirectly, what you infer from this logic? That, whatever religion that is based on "non-duality" is good for understanding the differences in human beings. So, now you know why Sanatana Dharma (whose principal ideas revolve around the "non-dualistic" or "advaitic" path) is the right one.

Our way of life is akin to science which is based on universal principles that are intrinsic to the functioning of the cosmos you have not understood me what I mean is Santana dharma is flexible and can adapt to new discoveries as science it is universal and is based on the rules on which life in this universe functions ! Saints in INDIA come and challenge the former and this is freedom to reform and perfect what we conceive, write and propagate. The content of dharma is updated by our Saints so this capacity flexibility, the ability to adapt to situations, going closer and closer to universal ethics and principles that are embedded in the secrets of creation. when I say we are the best, I mean whichever system which has the ability to reform itself is the best.

We have already "an open architecture " style "bank of knowledge" in which everyone can come and if he is convincing , Hindus adapt his ideas and integrate in what we call Hinduism (that word invented by invaders of INDIA which means "people living on the other side of the river Indus)..And why should we not clearly say that our path is the best ? we are not deriving undue pride but observing objectively the system allows flexibility and freedom that nowhere on earth we see so what see with our eyes , we say with our mouth and if you see anything close to this system , I am ready to examine. With globalisation and seeing how the western world materialistically rich (that too for 10%) but spiritually poor, we now can find in which place and position we can fit ourselves in considering the fabulous heritage we have. What is given importance in the west is Individualism, the desire to desire without shame of desiring without sharing and with the obsession to take all for oneself without giving anything to even an ant.

And in India we used to put aside individual pride and over bloated ego to think collectively. we don't have the same idea of DESIRE and consider that desire should be bound by borders of DHARMA.

what has done this immoral desire rather GREED and the over bloated ego cult in the west?

Individualistic and egoistic mind set makes a mother of two children choose a lover abandoning the children and husband because she gives priority to individual pleasure, "her egoistic pleasure" is more valuable to her eyes than her children being left like orphans and her husband left alone with them.

This same trait in the Europeans makes them go after a tennis player's win and celebrating a lonely sailor with a lonely boat proving to the French that an individual has succeeded in circumventing the globe alone in a boat! What is the necessity? THE EGO is their GOD. The French just prey it...Take the cycle tour of France, the formula 1 etc... The Individual success is glorified.

SINCE a few years, what started like a small fire is catching up the whole forest. What started as a small revolt by poor immigrants from North Africa is spreading all over there.

THEY target all these "super" "Hypermarchés" like CARREFOUR, AUCHAN, CHAMPION, CORA etc...

They protest against 10 percent of the French possessing 85 percent of Frances' land and money resources. The UN study confirms this gap between the haves and the have-nots. In the US, the gap is worst. A few hundred families own 80 percent of all-American resources.

Is this we want in India????

So, what is wrong in finding one's right place in the arena of nations by being true to own roots and heritage?

Why sculpting the inner mental statue is important? How an idea which got sowed inside becomes a tree in the external world? Eiffel tower before becoming a world wonder was an idea in a man's mind.

From what angle we see determines what aspects of things we see and we may conclude to act differently according to our perceptions.

Two angles may lead to two complete opposite conclusions.

Your vision differs as angles or positions changes.

India's strength is in the domain of the internal mind, the world of imagination, the perception of the invisible, the touching of the impalpable, being in union with the universal self-etc... This should not be taken for granted and should be protected as though they are visible heritage. The immaterial landscape of our internal mind when sculpted by a Vedic and Puranic education should be equally respected as any visible landscape of the material world.

Western people are astonished that they are incapable of apprehending what they cannot see. A cursory look of western people writing about our culture shows how they are wonderstruck by the intelligence of our ancestors.

We see what is invisible to the Westerners.

When we do Savahasana in Yoga, we send conscious orders mentally to our body to relax. In the west, only now they understand the virtue of what the French call "AUTO SUGGESTION".

They have also coined a word "sophrology" to copy this brilliant posture and prescribe "relaxation" (identical to this yogic posture) to people suffering from different psychosomatic disorders. A holistic study of a patient to treat his illness is the new idea in the west.

Likewise, they have done to Yoga and Pranayama which they call "cardiac coherence"! shameless copyists, cunning commercial-minded guys ! They won't even mention the source from where they borrowed and would make money shamelessly by stealing a "traditional knowledge" and corrupting it because they will never know how to do it according to the original TEXTS with guidance from authentic masters from Bharat, anyway.

A man of vision like Vajpayee conceived "the Golden Quadrilateral" as facilitating the circulation of persons and goods to make India a superpower and bring prosperity to millions by providing them with jobs while men of Greed who came to power after he left the government in May 2004 viewed this project only as a source of making money. The angle of one person brought prosperity while that of an immoral person caused calamities.

Now THAT IS WHY IT IS IMPORTANT TO EDUCATE CHILDREN AND HELP MORAL MINDSET EMERGE BY DESTROYING IMMORAL ONE. When SKANDA, DURGA, VISHNOU, SIVA fights against ASURAS, THIS IS THE ETERNAL BATTLE OF THE GOOD FIGHTING THE EVIL EVEN THOUGH THE WAR MAY SEEM ENDLESS AND THE GOD THEMSELVES MIGHT APPEAR TO LOSE HEART. In the end, we will learn that Dharma defeats Evil forces.

To underline this interior shakthi, take for example a TANJORE UNESCO CLASSIFIED SHIVA TEMPLE BUILT BY RAJA RAJA CHOZHA in ANKORVAT, IN CAMBODIA or this big "EIFFEL TOWER" IN PARIS.

What is exterior is only the idea once germinated like a seed in a human mind...A idea in its pure invisible form came up one day in the mind of this King Soja or this French architect in his dream...without this idea, no ANKORVAT TEMPLE IN CAMBODIA OR EIFFEL TOWER. We Indians are educators by excellence and sculptors of human mind...Certainly Puranas that I happened to hear from my grandfather are even now enchanting and giving me secretly lot of moral strength and pleasure.

Finally, what is the difference between Hitler and Gandhiji? That is the difference between one mind that has been trained to spread hatred and another that has learnt to spread love. The former used to listen to stories of crusaders, colonisers, looters and pirates while the latter was exposed to Puranas. That is the difference.

ANALYSING AN INFORAMTION FROM WESTERN MEDIA WITH CAUTION

There are two rules that we should apply before digesting information coming from external world. Why? Thanks to their money clout, big developed countries can buy corrupt people in high posts in any government of under developed or developing country.

So, let us be vigilant when we are presented with media news which are often news paid by some hidden people who direct the social mind-set in the way they want so that they can enhance their commercial gains or advance their political milestones.

RULE number 1: whatever the west ascertains as "rock», question its hardness and accept it only after thorough investigation.

RULE number 2: whoever the west promotes as "great" and cover him with NOBEL PRIZE, BEWARE! Do research on his past if he is truly worthy of all those praises because everything the west will do; it is for their "business" and never for a "selfless cause»; it is in their mind-set and I would say in their gene. Why? Because in the West, a few people (some bankers, industrialists, politicians and capitalists of all sorts) have succeeded in overpowering the majority; a mere 10% of them determine the fate of the rest of THE

SILENT MASSES. IT is just a closed knit community of wealthy oligarchy who have already tried their arms on their own citizens and then perfected those arms to such an extent that they do it in a «pavlovien" manner on the rest of the planet with a predilection for India, the potential and cultural clout of which they feel threatened. Their formula : media power + fashionable and spectacular events to promote their ideas like Nobel Prize + money clout + financing any future President whatever may be his party + collaborating with their Missionaries and sold-out politicians and NGO cum stooges to spread American culture depriving Indians completely of their "indianity" + selling all their goods to Indians who have lost their "indianity" Their goal is just commercial and JESUS is just one among ten means to attain that commercial goal !

Reading the history of the world, we incur that most of the genocide, invasions, wars, colonisation comes from the western world.

Why? This question is very important and needs to be answered after long reflection and meditation on the subject.

Why the western world is always seeing others as, if they happened to be human beings or animals, they should be exploited as a farmer would extract if he had a fruit in his hands?

Many reasons explain this instinct to survive: difficult cold climatic conditions, limited exposition to sun that constraints agriculture, search for spices to add to their insipid food, greed to get quickly rich by exploiting innocent people and animals, egoistic tendency to go after worldly materialistic pleasures, searching for joy outside oneself and never spending time on introspection and never searching for peace and joy inside our mental and spiritual space and last but not the least the monotheistic Abrahamic mindset.

Indian culture wants us to search for eternal, unfaltering and durable peace of mind inside us not outside us, in the material world as they are always subject to changes that are not under our control and thus, we cannot master them.

I will present this book like a menu in a restaurant: you will begin with an appetizer and proceed on to the main course and then will finish with a dessert.

The main course comprises of formulas that enemies of India, especially, the world new order club members from the west apply every time they want to control a given market and get a share of that market. Of course, the size of that share is directly proportionate to the depth of their greed!

THE MAIN COURSE:

Now that you have been introduced to the appetizer, we will go to the main course ...I AM GOING TO PUT MYSELF IN THE BODY OF THE GLOBAL INVISIBLE RULERS OF THE WEST AND RECOUNT A FASCINATING HISTORY OF THE WEST'S MURDEROUS ADVENTURES across Time and

Space. Let me become the white western who wanted to search for spices and instead of discovering INDIA touched the landmass which we now call "AMERICA" ...

I, the white American discovering America, think in the following manner:

Now that we have put all Red Indians in segregated zones as animals, now that we have made all black and creole inhabitants of SOUTH AMERICA a docile people by continuously keeping them brainwashed so that whatever they do, they do as their masters told them to do, we think we are already masters of the minds of people of South America and Africa with some exceptions. NOW THAT WE, WESTERN IMPERIALISTS HAVE MADE AFRICA ALMOST PREY LIKE US AND GIVE US FULL LIBERTY TO EXPLOIT, WITH NO CONCERN FOR THEIR ENVIRONMENT, THEIR GEOLOGICAL OR OCEAN RESOURCES AND CHINA AND INDIA HELP US TO PRODUCE MORE TO SELL TO THE REST OF THE PLANET, WE ALMOST CONTROL THE WHOLE WORLD.

BUT, SOME LEVEL OF OUR CONTROL OVER CHINA AND INDIA MAY VARY:

CHINA EMULATES OUR CAPITALIST SYSTEM MARVELLOUSLY WELL ALL BY THEIR OWN WILL, KILLING THEIR TRADITIONAL WAY OF LIVING, THUS PASSING ON THEIR OWN WILL, A SUICIDE ROPE AROUND THEIR NECK,

BUT, ALTHOUGH ECONOMICALLY THEY HAVE BECOME UNWILLINGLY OUR SLAVE, THEY AT LEAST CONSERVE A DISTINCTIVE LINGUISTIC DIFFERENCE, INDIA HAS NOT EVEN THIS LANGUAGE BARRIER FOR US TO INVADE THEIR PSYCHE. THANKS TO OUR BRITISH ANCESTORS WHO MADE THEM EXTERNALLY INDIAN BUT INTERNALLY SO BRITISH. IN THIS SCENARIO, WHICH PLACE RUSSIA FITS IN? RUSSIA IS NOT TOTALLY FOLLOWING OUR ECONOMIC MODEL EVEN THOUGH BILLIONAIRES FROM THEIR COUNTRY IS ON THE INCREASE (GOOD NEWS FOR US. WE HOPE WITH ALL FRENCH LUXURY GOING IN MOSCOW TO MAKE THEM GREEDY LIKE US FOR USELESS GOODS, THEY MAY FOLLOW OUR MODEL IN THE LONG TERM AND JOIN US BECOMING A

SATELLITE LIKE CHINA OR JAPAN), THEY ARE STILL POSING MANY PROBLEMS FOR THE WESTERN TO APPREHEND AND COMPREHEND, AT LEAST IN THE SHORT TERM. THEIR LINGUISTIC AND CLIMATIC CONDITIONS MAKE THEM A NON-REACHABLE ZONE FOR THE WESTERN IMPERIALIST EAGLE AND ITS SNIFFING DOGS.

COMING TO INDIA, EVEN THOUGH INDIANS SPEAK ENGLISH BUT YET THEY ARE DIFFICULT TO UNDERSTAND. WE THINK INDIA HAS A GREAT CULTURAL HERITAGE THANKS TO HER ANCIENT CIVILISATION THAT CAN COMPLICATE IN OUR PROSELYTING MISSION AND CAN EVEN POSE A THREAT FOR OUR MONOTHEISTIC RELIGION IN THE LONG RUN BY PROPOSING A CHOICE TO HUMANITY OF A BETTER ALTERNATIVE. BY THE BY, HERE IS THE TRUTH ABOUT OUR IDEA OF RELIGION: WE THINK RELIGION SHOULD BE A POLITICAL INSTRUMENT TO ATTAIN MATERIAL GOALS, THAT 'S ALL. NO SENTIMENTS LIKE INDIANS WHO PREY GANGA RIVER.

BY THE BY, WE ACCUSE THEM OF IDOLATRY AND LAUGH AT THEIR FOLLY OF PANTHEISTIC RELIGION.

(WE KNOW THAT HINDUS DON'T PREY DIRECTLY TO A STONE STATUE BUT THROUGH THAT STATUE, THEY MEDITATE UPON THE UNIVERSAL FORMLESS ENERGY WHICH EXPRESSES ITSELF THROUGH ALL CREATION AND FORMS. BUT, LET US PRETEND WE DO NOT KNOW ALL THIS SO THAT WE CAN CONTINUE TO MAKE FUN OF THEM AND HARVEST SOULS FOR OUR MIDDLE-EAST GOD CHRIST EXPORTED TO COLD SNOW-CLAD PAGAN EUROPE AND RUSSIA FROM A HOT DESERT AS A GIFT! IN WHOSE NAME, WE COMMITTED GENOCIDE IN NORTH AND SOUTH AMERICA TO AFRICA VIA INDIA. (HERE IS THE TRUE IMAGE OF JESUS thanks to CNN:

WE SELLERS OF GOODS TO THE WORLD ARE AFRAID THAT IF AT ALL PEOPLE IN THE WEST AND THE EAST EMBRACE SANATANA DHARMA, THEY MAY BE MORE CAREFUL ABOUT ECOLOGICAL CONCERNS AS HINDUS RESPECT EARTH AS MOTHER.

THEIR SINCERE AFFECTION FOR ALL LIVING BEINGS INCLUDING ANIMALS PREVENT OUR MEAT INDUSTRY TO EXPAND AND THEIR SINCERE PAGAN

CONCERN FOR THE ENVIRONMENT PREVENT OUR MINING AND ENERGY INDUSTRY TO CONTINUE WITH THEIR MINDLESS EXPLOITATION. THEIR ATTACHMENT TO A MORE TRADITIONAL AGRICULTURE PREVENTS US TO SELL THEM GMO FOODS AND OTHER JUNK FOODS AND DIABETIC COCA AND MAKE THEM OBESE LIKE US.

THEIR ATTACHMENT TO A MORE SINCERE AND SOLID FAMILY STRUCTURE PREVENT US TO SELL THEM ALL OUR USELESS MAKE-UP AND OTHER HIGH-HEELS ETC SO THAT THEIR WOMEN MAY ALSO BECOME LIKE OUR LADIES AFRAID OF BEING NATURAL AND LESS FAMILY CARING AND MORE PRONE TO DELEGATE THEIR KITCHEN WORK TO CARELESS AND CYNIC INDUSTRIALISTS!

WHEN INDIANS HAD FINISHED EATING ALL OUR JUNK FOODS, WE ARE READY TO GIVE THEM OUR MEDICINE.

ALAS! INDIA HAS YOGA AND AYURVEDIC MEDICAL SYSTEM WHICH BASED ON HOLISTIC AND HERBAL REMEDIES, CAN POSE A THREAT TO OUR MEDICAL SYSTEM IN THE LONG RUN.

SO, WE ARE PUSHED TO COPY AND PATENT WHATEVER THEIR CIVILISATION HAD PRODUCED BY SAYING THAT AS WE MADE SOME ALTERATIONS, THAT MAKES THAT YOGA DIFFERENT OR THEIR AYURVEDA, SIDDHA MEDICINE COMPLETELY AMERICAN. WE ARE ALREADY PATENTING WHATEVER WE FIND INTERESTING IN THEIR PLANTS AND HERBS AND OTHER INTERESTING NATURAL BIOLOGICAL DIVERSITY OF ASIA AND AFRICA SO THAT THEY WILL HAVE TO PAY TO USE THEIR OWN NATURAL REMEDIES MADE FROM PLANTS GROWING ONLY IN THEIR LANDS.

SO, THEIR ANCIENT CULTURE AND THEIR WAY OF LIVING IS OUR ENEMY AND WE WILL BREAK THAT BY PROSELYTING THEM WITH our imported DESERT MAN JESUS WHO IS DEPICTED AS "BLOND WITH BLUE EYES" WRONGLY so as to flatter our ego of WHITE PEOPLE.

TO BEGIN, WE CAN JUST BREAK INDIA IN TO SMALL REGIONS SO THAT IT MAY NEVER BECOME A COUNTER-POWER WHERE SOFTWARE AND

HARDWARE ARE PRODUCED MORE EFFECTIVELY THAN IN OUR OWN WESTERN COUNTRIES.

FOR US RELIGION IS JUST AN INSTRUMENT TO ATTAIN OUR COMMERCIAL AND MATERIAL DESIRES. We are cold and calculated and these two qualities define our CIA.

BUT WE ARE CONFUSED TO SEE THAT FOR INDIA, IT IS NOT SO. THEY PUT DESIRES FOR MATERIALS IN THE BACKYARD.

MOREOVER, WE WOULD LIKE INDIA TO FOLLOW OUR MONOTHEISTIC APPROACH TO RELIGION BECAUSE, THAT MAY FACILITATE TO UNDERSTAND THEIR MINDS.

TO BE ABLE TO SELL TO A COUNTRY, WE SHOULD BE ABLE TO UNDERSTAND THEIR DEEP PSYCHE. IF THEY ARE TOO CONSCIOUS THAT MATERIAL DESIRE ALONE IS NOT THE ULTIMATE GOAL OF LIFE, THEN THAT DIVERGENT BEHAVIOUR CAN NOT FACILITATE A BETTER PENETRATION OF THEIR MARKETS. IF YOU DON'T GIVE IMPORTANCE TO SUPERFLUOUS DESIRES, WE CAN SELL NOTHING TO YOU! We would do all kinds of tricks so that you copy our consumerism of useless scents and cigarettes!

SO, WE WESTERN POWERS, FEEL IT IS BETTER TO BREAK INDIA AND CONTROL THEM SO THAT THEY HAVE NO ALTERNATIVE SYSTEM TO PROPOSE EITHER TO OUR CAPITALISM OR TO OUR RELIGION.

HOW DO WE DO ALL THIS SUBVERSIVE ACTS: GIVE A FORMER PRESIDENT'S WIFE (HILARY CLINTON) THE POWER TO MANAGE A TRUST IN WHICH ALL MNCs WILL POUR MONEY. MAINTAIN THE NETWORK OF THE BIG NEXUS BETWEEN CIA - INDUSTRIALISTS- NGOs- CHURCH-POLITICIANS WORK IN TANDEM TO EXECUTE THE GRAND DESTINY OF THE WESTERN WORLD: TO RULE THE WORLD. THANKS TO CLINTON-LIKE PEOPLE. Our missionaries had done a great job and now we have Indian Christians helping us with proselytization: we now can send our boys infiltrate even Hindu Parties like B.J.P.

HERE IS THE FORMULA we WESTERN POWER, UNDECLARED AND SECRET PREDATOR AND ENEMY OF INDIAN CIVILISATION AND CULTURAL

HERITAGE, TO DIVIDE AND BREAK INDIA. (I BEGAN TO WRITE THIS ESSAY WHEN THE DIABOLIC DUO "SONIA -MANMOHAN" WERE IN POWER AND NOW IT IS UPDATED ON 9th JUNE OF 2014). AFTER MODIJI WAS ELECTED WITH ABSOLUTE MAJORITY. TROJAN HORSES AND SECRET SPIES WHO BREAK INDIA WILL HAVE A DIFFICULT TIME WITH MODI NOW THAT HE IS GIVEN FULL POWER BY THE INDIAN VOTERS, NEVERTHELESS, WE SHOULD CONTINUE TO BE VIGILANT.

READING THE BELOW LIST OF METHODS THAT OUR ENEMIES EMPLOY TO BREAK US MAY BE USEFUL TO KEEP THAT VIGILANCE LAMP ALWAYS LIT, ALIVE AND BRIGHT.

We should know that in spite of the fact that there are many brands, most of the time they belong to one big group! We, consumers, have an illusion of choice but the majority of brands belong to few companies.

FORMULA 1)

CONTROL INDIAN MIND BY MACAULAY TYPE OF EDUCATION in SCHOOLS RUN BY MISSIONARIES FROM USA.

By education, media, audio-visual and cinematographic propaganda, people's mind can also be easily colonized. So, the formula of our enemies is:

Make them cook, eat, taste, dress, dance, speak, sing, smoke and drink like us;

Make them enjoy and like and dislike the same things we do;

Make the architects of INDIA think adopt a "pensée unique" approach for building construction in terms of cement and sand and never make them go back to those noble NATURAL materials that resist naturally sun rays of the tropics like bamboo or other agricultural by-products that Indian ancestors once used so wisely to alleviate the hot sun rays' bad effects and more adapted to their tropical climate. Make them our silent followers so that they may continue to siphon sand from all their sea shores that is copying our mindset; "take always from earth continuously but never give back, because our greed is fathomless as ocean."

Make them think and dream like us even though they may not look like us and the colour of their skin may be black or yellow, if they think and live like us, we can happily go on selling them what we produce, that is the only thing important and for that, we can go to any extent.

In the process of colonizing minds of the target country's people, if we can take their gold, silver, titanium, thorium, rare metals, petrol, gas or anything their land may contain under its surface, well, we will invent any pretext to bomb or steal that wealth in stealth.

Unfortunately, powerful country like RUSSIA's rich gas remains out of our greedy bear claws' reach but how to seize it is still a problem for us. We also have more difficulty to penetrate and spy them, they are linguistically and culturally so different like those Chinese! Happily, thanks to English colonisation, Indians at least are easy to manage. Let us hope so.

Above all, let us plunder India's ancient sacred culture and eat and digest their priceless value system and beliefs so that we may boast that all that culture is ours' and we can accuse them by saying that it is they who stole that cultural heritage from us when, in reality, it is we who stole from them !

Make them believe that their culture and religion is inferior in quality, baseless, superstitious, foolish and what not, so that they may abandon their religion and convert to ours'.

Make them think very low of whatever their ancestors had produced so that they will abandon all the wisdom from their ancestors and embrace western way of living as a fanatic consumerist who can no more think of a world without hyper markets covering hectares of surface.

Go on taking from the earth whatever it may contain under it's surface without ever giving back anything in return. Grateful indeed these greedy guys are to the Mother Nature!

MAKE INDIAN FARMERS QUIT THEIR VILLAGES AND INDUCE THEM TO SEARCH FOR JOBS IN INDUSTRIES IN URBAN CITIES.

WE like the word "concentration" and apply it to our production sites that produce and our storerooms that store them and hypermarkets that sell them to urban cities with dense population of readily available clients for our goods. This is our virtuous circle that can be a "vicious» one for others.

(This is my humble request to our Prime Minister. Please MODIJI sir, please don't listen to World Bank which wants our farmers quit villages and overcrowd our urban cities so that they may become a ready-made client for their industrial products. when farmers leave their job of cultivating of India, when their land is bought by real estate companies, food production will fall and will not feed our population, so we will have to import industrially produced grains by American or European farming corporates there by becoming beggars with a begging bowl for our daily food, that will create a dependence worse than when we depended upon the British colonial masters for our livelihood.)

MAKE them build urban gigantic cities and create concentration of people in those cities paving way for an easy market penetration of western products.

FORMULA 2)

CONTROL INDIAN MIND BY PAID USA MEDIA WORKING IN INDIA OR WITH THE HELP OF AN INNOCENT LOOKING NGO SPREADING CULTURE

OR THANKS TO AN ENTERTAINMENT COMPANY LIKE THAT OF RUPERT MURDOCH, THE MEDIA BARON OF STAR TV, VIJAY TV AND OTHER MEDIA HOUSES. THE TAMIL NADU HAS ALSO THEIR LOCAL MASS MIND POLLUTER LIKE SUN TV. BESIDES WE WANT TO CONTROL CULTURE, VALUES and HABITS BY MNC IN NEXUS WITH OUR PROTESTANT AND VATICAN CHURCH.

FORMULA 3)

CONTROL STANDARDS OF MORALITY WITH HUMAN RIGHTS, NOBEL AND OTHER PRICE GIVING TRUSTS FIXING THE STANDARD OF WHAT IS WORTHY OF GETTING REWARDED AND WHAT IS NOT WORTHY, ALWAYS ACCORDING TO WESTERN

STANDARDS, SPREAD REVOLUTIONS AND SPRING
UPRISING IN ARAB AND ASIA BY SPREADING
SECRETLY CIA FUNDED NGOS.

N.B: I am very happy to learn this great man Shri
Kailash Satyarthi had been bestowed upon with
the Nobel price. But I feel that western people
have too much blood of innocent North and South
American Indians and Africans in their hands. They
invented slavery in its most cruel form and
unleashed injustice in all their erstwhile colonies
including India, They don't deserve to give prizes in
the name of peace India is better placed to
dispense this price; Even though Sweden is a
neutral country and had never been directly
implicated in wars , this prize is showcased as
"WESTERN" . We need to create a GANDHIJI prize
and that should become the global benchmark for
evaluating someone's service for peace; We are
the nation who invented non-violent methods to
win a war and the western people have no merit
to hijack a global peace cause.

CONTROL MONEY WITH INTERNATIONAL BANKS LIKE WORLD BANK AND INTERNATIONAL MONETARY FUND (http://panindiahindu.blogspot.com/2014/06/the-imfs-emphasis-on-macroeconomic.html) AND BY LOANS WITH DRACONIAN CONDITIONS FAVORING AMERICAN FORTUNE 500 PEOPLE ...FIRST LEND THEM AND THEN BEND THEM TO YOUR DESIRE. FORCE AND THREATEN THEM TO OPEN INDIA's MARKET MAKING INDIANS JOBLESS WHILE ENRICHING THOSE WESTERN INVESTORS WHOSE PREDATION ON EMERGING MARKETS KEEP THEIR OVEN HOT. Privatization and opening Indian market for the foreign MNC vultures such as WALMART AND CARREFOUR WERE THE DEMANDS OF THIS DIRTY BANK. On the pressure of the World Bank, Indian corrupt politicians are pressuring the common man who retorts by rejecting them in elections.

WHY THE FRENCH HOTEL GROUP ACCOR CAN GO ON BUILDING HOTELS IN INDIA BUT NOT EVEN TATA IS ABLE TO BUY ASSETS IN FRANCE?

WHY FRENCH COMPANIES LIKE ALCATEL, ALSTOM, AREVA, DASSAULT, EADS, EDF, GAZ DE FRANCE AND THALES RUSH TO BUY SPACE IN DELHI WHILE AN INDIAN LIKE LAKSHMI MITAL WHEN HE WANTED TO ENTER THE FRENCH IRON AND STEEL SECTOR BY BUYING ARCELOR MITAL WAS PUT TO INDIAN BASHING BY FRENCH SOCIETY IN GENERAL AND FRENCH MEDIA IN PARTICULAR. THE RACIST REMARKS AGAINST LAKSHMI MITAL SHOULD NOT BE TOLERATED AND EVERY INDIAN SHOULD MAKE SURE THAT FRENCH COMPANIES GET THE SAME TREATMENT HERE AND WE SHOULD MAKE THEM QUIT IF THEY DON' T OPEN THEIR MARKET AS FREELY AS WE DO TO THEM. Reciprocity should be the general rule.

FORMULA 5)

38

CONTROL BLACK MONEY TAPS WITH KICKBACKS BY "GOVT TO GOVT" SALES OF ARMS BY EXCHANGING COMMISSIONS IN DOLLARS BETWEEN HEAD OF COUNTRIES WHO SELL AND BUY SUCH ARMS.

INDIAN CONGRESS PARTY'S HEAD IS MRS SONIA GANDHI, AN ITALIAN LADY WHO ENTERED THE GANDHI FAMILY BY MARRYING THE SON OF INDIRA GANDHI, THE LATE MR RAJIV GANDHI. SHE RULED INDIA BY NAMING A PUPPET CALLED MANMOHAN SINGH AS PRIME MINISTER, WHO SAID "AMEN" TO HER TO ANYTHING SHE SAID AND WANTED. WHAT SHE DID IS JUST FOR 10 YEARS WAS FULFILLING THE EVANGELISTS AGENDA. SHE HAS BECOME ONE OF THE RICHEST POLITICIANS IN THE WORLD BY STEALING INDIAN TAXPAYERS' MONEY. SHE SYSTEMATICALLY GOT KICKBACKS FOR ALL SALES OF ARMAMENTS FROM FOREIGN COUNTRIES.

FORMULA 6)

CONTROL WORLD TRADE BY AMERICAN DOMINATED WORLD TRADE ORGANISATION BY HAND TWISTING AND FORCING BANANA REPUBLIC MINISTERS WHO LIKE TO GET SOME KICKBACKS.

See what the erstwhile imperial FRANCE does in THE TAHITI AND NEO CALEDONIAN ISLANDS and judge for yourself if they acted according to dharma or not:

Chaotic History of FRANCE in their colonies.

New Caledonia witnesses still a discord and some decades before, there developed a "war like situation " when the canaks and the French openly attacked each other but the tribal people had almost succeeded in making Jacques CHIRAC, the then French President , give them a "quasi" independent status with a locally elected government (in fine, it was under French control) .. There also, they stole the nickel, the biggest reserve of the world in nickel is in New Caledonia. And a French company was given "carte blanche" to do whatever they want, destroying the aborigine's culture. I just remember another serious matter they did there: explode a nuclear bomb for a test while they will never dare to even think of that on their land. They come here 12000 kms away from France near TAHITI, they explode a nuclear bomb and then go back safely while all the Indian ocean including India, I suspect, could have been exposed to high radioactivity. This will be never known to the outside world had they not sunk a "Greenpeace" boat and killed the protesting innocent guys.

They do not care about your attachment to your local culture and do not care whether you speak mahorais, canak, african tribal etc ; whatever race you may belong to, whatever social fabric you may have woven and created a unique culture, they don't care ; they just want to govern , rule their land by putting in place their government as they did in MAYOTTE, because they have a unquenchable thirst for power , money and resources of other innocent people whom they will keep under their colonial strict control

They are also very proud of the result of such a not so enviable action: Black Africans behaving like they are Europeans under the tropical sun of Martinique or Guadeloupe or The Reunion ISLAND.

All this because of their small geographical and demographical size, they feel such an inferiority complex that they want to still maintain cunningly their grip over these African populated islands...!

TRUTH may be hard to digest but if you digest it will give you peps that will make you stronger than ever before!

FORMULA 7)

CONTROL THROUGH CIA AND DIPLOMATIC CHANNELS PEOPLE IN HIGH POLITICAL POSITIONS. (In 1700, ROBERT CLIVE USED INDIANS (SEPOYS) to control INDIANS.

From 2004 till MAY 2014, AN ITALIAN USED INDIANS (CONVERTED INDIAN CHRISTIANS AND PRIESTS) TO DIVIDE AND PROSELYTIZE INDIANS AND DESTROY THE VERY CULTURAL FOUNDATION OF INDIA.
(http://panindiahindu.blogspot.com/2014/06/a-hindu-argues-circles-around.html)

BEFORE, THE BRITISH WANTED ONLY TO CONTROL INDIA POLITICALLY AND COMMERCIALLY BUT THE ITALIAN LADY WANTED TO USE MONEY TO BUY THEIR SOULS AND BURN THEM IN HELL. SHE USED THE SAME FORMULA: ENSLAVE INDIANS CULTURALLY AND SPIRITUALLY BY EMPLOYING INDIAN PRIESTS AND BISHOPS.

Just Google FORD FOUNDATION IN INDIA. You will be stunned to learn that the USA is funding a new political party and promoting it with "dollar force" by buying massive Media support for making the American Party in Indian dress a success. Instead of wasting their time to buy out Indian politicians, they now fund people who create new INDIAN POLITICAL PARTIES as they funded NGOS run by

AAM ADMI PARTY leader KEJERWAL so as to indirectly help him create this American remote-controlled Indian Party. Imagine if such a party can win elections and become big enough to govern

India. That will make INDIA the worst banana republic on earth! (visit my blog whose link is below :
http://panindiahindu.blogspot.com/2014/06/foreign-aided-ngos-are-actively.html)

FORMULA 8)

CONTROL DEMOGRAPHY BY FORCED MASS CONVERSIONS TO CREATE CAPTIVE CLIENTS TO THE USA MNCs AND BUY DIRECTLY PEOPLE IN INDIAN BUREAU OF INTELLIGENCE AS IN THE CASE OF NAMBI NARAYANAN, A TRUE PATRIOT WHOSE DESIRE TO COMPETE WITH USA by MAKING GSLV ROCKET COSTED HIM DEARLY. THANKS TO RUSSIA, INDIA COULD MAKE PROGRESS IN CRYOGENIC ROCKET IN SPITE OF AMERICAN SANCTIONS). BY the by, western Imperialists sent mercenaries of Indian origin to kill the Indian scientists working in Rocket launching who may pose a threat to American and European scientific and commercial monopoly in rocket or nuclear technology.

FORMULA 9)

CONTROL POLITICIANS BY LURING THEM with SEXY JOURNALISTS UNDER THE PRETEXT OF INTERVIEWING THEM AND BLACKMAILING THEM AFTERWARDS.

FORMULA 9) MAKE INDIANS ADOPT OUR AMERICAN NAMES LIKE DAVID , JOHN OR JOSEPH ETC This is "CULTURAL RAPE : Control by penetrating Indian cinema world to persuade famous ACTORS to change their Hindu names to Christian names (a cursory investigation by a journalist may reveal fantastic scoops)..It may seem petty but by drop by drop the poison may pollute the whole society. It is a way of getting the access to the collective consciousness of Indians who seeing actors with names like David may finally lift their guard and accept those names in the long run and may even give them to their children. (I call this colonizing the collective consciousness). Why they want to colonize something invisible inside you? Because, the more you accept them, the more they can harvest "souls" for their JESUS, the middle-east man whose looks are like that of a north European. IT IS THIS THEY WANT: ACCEPTABILITY. Their long-term recolonization of India should first begin by making a white alien Vatican culture familiar to you. Acceptability is the key to your heart and purse.

https://www.youtube.com/watch?v=X6LQkWwQrZU

Go to this link on acceptability: (http://panindiahindu.blogspot.com/2014/02/acceptability-is-key-to-your-heart-and.html).

FORMULA 10

MAKE INDIANS ACCEPT OUR CHURCH IN THEIR CITIES : This is " GEOGRAPHICAL RAPE" ; Control the geographical relief of a city or a village by inserting the church in that milieu , this is also similar to the above process ; only instead of a name getting access to the collective OK of a society , it is a place which gets that collective OK because of its strategic situation being in the middle of a busy place where people pass constantly from four directions and they will finish by accepting a church "unconsciously" as a thing of their internal memory of the geography of their town...this is another kind of "colonizing" the internal memory of a person without his permission. So, it is a kind of rape and subduing the mind of a person when he is the least alert.

+ European media only insists on rapes in India which is statistically a ridiculous thing when you compare with the 1 billion population in India where as in Europe and in the USA, it is many times superior to the numbers of Indian crimes! But they want to stop Santana Dharma getting stronger and challenging conversion by CHRISTIANITY. So, they try to link Hinduism with all this "rape mentality" that shows that woman is not respected in Hindu culture so "come to my religion".

FORMULA 11)

Control universities and centres of education by hiding behind the noble cause of education the mission to convert innocent students to Christianity, dispense false doctorates in Hinduism whose mission would be to publish false information on Hinduism and especially by proposing courses in media management and technology that may be useful to reinforce the control. THIS SEPOY PLANTING IN FOREIGN COUNTRIES ALSO IS A WELL OILED MECHANISM THAT HAS TRAITORS FOR DOING IGNOMINIOUS JOB OF MUDSLINGING ON HINDU LEADERS,

WATCH OUT THIS SEPOY WHOSE NAME IS MEENA DHANDA,,WHO SEEMS TO POSE A SERIOUS THREAT TO HINDUISM , They are criminals whose main MISSION is "intellectual contamination" of people against Hinduism and its supporters and followers, People like MEENA DHANDA are recruited for "Hindu bashing" and their mission is to contaminate intellectually the scientific community with essays to discredit Hindu leaders. We should also understand that in Universities world over, professors are recruited to this anti-India subversive activities and they form a big international network working in unison and tandem with AAP leader ARAVIND KEJRIVAL, her colleagues are those who succeeded in setting up Trojan horses in INDIA in the name of "AAP party». She praises only those AAP traitors waiting to be tried for treason who got elected in PUNJAB. SHE IS A "Sepoy" PROFESSOR IN UP. Now it is clear, AAP is a criminal international network working in unison and in tandem to destroy Hinduism. (http://panindiahindu.blogspot.com/2014/06/will-govt-dismantle-large-complex-anti.html)

For example, The New York Times often ask people who hate India like PANKAJ MISHRA to write hateful things on India so that they cannot be taxed as racist. If you can't be overtly racist and negative on India, the next best thing to do is to get a disgruntled Indian intellectual, someone cut off from his roots, to do the job. No one can then accuse you of racism.

FORMULA 12).

Control by issuing an identity bio-metric card (happily MR NANDAN NILEKANI who worked in this bio-metric project, lost his election) for every Indian so that everything about his personal data may be readily available for CIA; If at all any Indian thinks ill of Uncle Sam in any way, his freedom of expression may be curtailed via internal powerful politicians on USA payroll or direct commando forces. At the end of the day, that could be helpful to demographically determine where Christian population is needed to increase so as to reap not only souls but also electoral gains.

FORMULA 13).

Give money to crooked "scientists" and ask them to deliver bulshit that is "bogus studies" and make it sensational in all media to make it sound like a stupendous "discovery" of the century to demonize a respectable civilization like "Indus Valley Civilization".

Spread lies through fabricating fake theories like the Aryan invasion theory of India.

MICHEL DANINO, a French scholar debunked this fake theory according to which Vedic literature was brought by some Indo-Europeans called "Aryan" when they entered India crossing the river INDUS.

But, in RIG VEDA they mention a mythic river called "saraswati" that existed before the arrival of the so-called Aryans! so, how could they write about a river which existed before 2000 years if they came to India 500 years after that river dried up????

FORMULA 14).

If some Indian philosopher like TIROUVALUVAR seems to be outstandingly intelligent then say Saint Thomas or some x saint passed by CHENNAI where he was living and inspired TITOUVALUVAR to write all the poems so brilliantly applauded by the public. Same thing as above for MS SUBULAKSHMI a great Carnatic singer was photographed with Pope and was taken to Vatican by a local Bishop to confuse innocent minds. In that photo, poor MS SUBULAKSHMI innocently posed beside Pope as a goat beside a Tiger... That photo was meant to show to future Tamil converts that even their elitist Tamil Carnatic singer is compatible with POPE culture!

FORMULA 15)

SEND ARMIES OF MISSIONARIES TO THE TRIBAL AREAS AND EXPLOITING THE INNOCENCE OF TRIBALS' hospitality, convert them and make them fight against themselves ... (The northeast region has become so infected by Christian militants and conversions that they want to secede from the rest of India and become their own Christian country, against the wishes of those who want to remain a part of the Vedic or indigenous cultures.).

WHEN WILL THIS "MY GOD IS THE BEST " MINDSET WILL CEASE TO EXIST AND GIVE WAY TO A MORE HEALTHEIR HOLLISTIC VISION THAT IS SCIENTIF IN TEMPER LIKE THE VISION WHICH IS PRONED BY SANATANA DHARMA ??

FORMULA 16)

WE the oligarchy 1% of the US WANTED TO STOP MODI FROM BECOMING PRIME MINISTER OF INDIA. Why ?

We perceived in him someone who is patriotic and pro-Indian not "boughtable" and "corruptible" as would like THE QUEEN OF AMERICA HILARY CLINTON... BUT ALAS ALL OUR EFFORTS HAVE FAILED BECAUSE INDIANS MASSIVELY ELECTED HIM AND BY ELECTING HIM, THEY SUPPORT HIS LOVE FOR HINDUISM. HERE IS WHAT WE TRIED TO DO, without any success, SO THAT PEOPLE MAY NOT ELECT HIM:

CONDEMN MODI AND DO TO DAMAGE HIS RAISING AS THE FUTURE LEADER OF INDIA

BECAUSE HE WILL CREATE A NEW INDIA PROUD OF HERSELF SO LET HE BE CRUSHED IN THE BEGINNING ITSELF AS THE PLANT WHEN IT BECOMES TREE WILL BE DIFFICULT TO CUT DOWN BUT THE FATE DECIDED OTHERWISE AND NOW IN 2019 HE HAS BECOME THE PRIME MINISTER OF INDIA.

Modiji, the present PRIME MINISTER OF INDIA, a man of ethics combated his enemies with "dharma" as his weapon while his enemies branded "cunningness and crookedness "as their arms. But dharma won when the whole Indian people elected him as their PRIME MINISTER OF INDIA in spite of all conspiracies thrown on him. officially by US PARLIAMENT for false accusation of genocide of Muslims by Hindus under his government in GUJARAT;

WHATEVER cunning conspiracies we may do outside America, we will ensure that American silent masses are not aware of any of our mischiefs in those parts of the world!

FORMULA 17)

Through organisations like HUMAN RIGHTS OR USCIRF, which was created by evangelical members of Congress with the initial intent of securing Christians, we should pretend to be victims and lash out pro-Hindu politician and paint him as black as possible so that he will never win an election. USCIRF Vice Chair Katrina Lantos Swett zealously lashes out at Modi at numerous fora, and even said that she hoped that her criticisms of Modi would serve as a 'bit of information that will help Indian voters as they go through that electoral process.' (http://panindiahindu.blogspot.com/2014/05/it-was-as-if-script-of-crime-was.html).

FORMULA 18)

In ancient times, India witnessed British using Indian soldiers against Indians. Now, Christian militants use Indian and Asian and even African pastors to convert Indians. This technique to control Indians by Indians is what I call "sepoy strategy". From the colonisation of AFRICA , from the way even a tiny country of the size of CHIDAMBARAM in TAMIL NADU like BELGIUM can do such atrocities in CONGO , from the way a country like FRANCE which has the size of TAMIL NADU exploited , tortured people in ALGERIA, morocco, Tunisisa, SENEGAL, mali, Niger, Tchad, Centrafrique, Cameroun, Gabon et à Pondichéry, Reunion, cambodia, Indochine, Vietnam, NEO CALAEDONIA, and the way Hitler handled the Jews, we can safely conclude that Abrahamic religion has something weird built in it that drives the people insane.

FORMULA 19)

SPY INDIA FROM THE SKIES:

Integrate technology and armament to consolidate political power by overpowering countries as if to tell them, "your geography is naked to us and we know all your strengths and weaknesses so that we can win over you in any war, be careful" ...From 1966 until its last mission in 1989, the Lockheed SR-71 Blackbird flew thousands of missions around the globe, photographing military installations from India to Egypt including China and the Arctic Circle to North Korea. If USA can do it to other countries, why others could not do the same to them? So, don't be the first to pollute minds with "conquering or fear mind-set" the two are two faces of the same coin. Don't live in eternal fear of being attacked...Live according to DHARMA.

FORMULA 20)

INDUSTRIES IN THE US BECOMING BIGGER THAN THEIR GOVERNMENT; MNCs had become slowly parallel governments controlling democratically elected government. When they grow in size with a budget higher than that of the nation in which they are implanted, than it is high time to regulate them and contain their corrupt practices. Better, the government should enact laws to determine the size of MNCs that will allow just to be profitable without the power to corrupt. Big is not always synonymous to beautiful. The more the economic crisis grips Industrialists, the more their LOBBYING gets intense. Since the World War II, defiance manufacturing is the biggest manufacturing industry of the US and its biggest employer. GE is one of the flagship companies in its stable. However, these war factories thrive on the sadistic creation of anarchy in nations particularly far from the shores of the US.

In India, GE is engaged in dubious activities that are blatantly anti-India by supporting financially Medias whose shareholders are illegal Christian missionaries with sole activity is Hindu mudslinging.

GE's involvement with NDTV, a news media with Christian missionary's capital, is particularly shocking and a gross infringement on the sovereignty of India; a grave, shocking and criminal act deserving severe retaliation and a thorough probe by our intelligence agencies.

GE has been severely indicted by the Dispute Resolution Panel (DRP) of the Income Tax department for having made shady and dubious investments to the tune of USD 150 million or Rs. 642.54 crores at 2008 – 09 valuations into an NDTV subsidiary. This entire amount has been declared as a "sham transaction" by the DRP.

Why would GE an AMERICAN COMPANY had freehand with Indian congress party's help to make investments in an INDIAN national news channel like NDTV which people think is 100% Indian while the truth is by way of dubious and illegal investments, USA's INDUSTRIAL GIANT G.E HAD TOOK 100% CONTROL OF AN INDIAN NATIONAL MEDIA ...WHAT IS THE OBJECTIVE BEHIND THIS SUBVERSIVE ACT ? Was it for illegal bribes? Was it to buy politicians? Was it to influence public opinion?

Now, the history had changed since 2019 and NDTV 's chief corrupt majority shareholder PRANOY ROY was asked to step down lest he will feel the heat of the judiciary.

FORMULA 21)

SEND ARMIES OF NGOS TO POLLUTE THE TARGET COUNTRY THAT YOU THINK IS NOT BENDING LOW TO YOUR FEET AND POLISH YOUR SHOES:

Hillary Clinton liked to operate through NGOs which are based in Scandinavian countries rather than American NGOS because NGOs based in Netherlands, Denmark and Norway do not attract attention from big power pollical entities.

The fact that these NGOs were vocal in protesting against Russia baked nuclear plant in Kudankulam is because the business in FRANCE is affected so France was trying to pressurise indirectly India to abandon cooperation with Russia and buy Areva company reactors. These NGOS were sent to GUJARAT also to incriminate somehow NARENDRA MODI in some kind of crime thinking that they may tumble upon some mass graves but without success. They only ended up in finding some buffaloes bones in an open field after searching for mass graves for more than 6 years!

There are some 30,81,873 NGOs in INDIA...! why do we need so many NGOs???

There are some important questions that may arise in the mind of any man of the street; these are the following:

Imagine just ₹ One Lakh allocation for each NGO by Indian government!

Enormous amount of Govt money get siphoned by these NGOs...!

And most of these NGOs get money from foreign agencies too...!

Are they not modern spies employed by the foreign agencies?

Is it not true that most NGOs act against India's national interest? Are they not utilised for conversions?

Is it not true that most money is utilised to propagate communal division and caste division?

Is it not true that most NGOs flare up anti-Govt sentiments and instigate public?

Is it not true that most NGOs assist the terrorists and Naxalites?

Most often Indian pastors and fathers are employed as COOLIES to garner foolish people as members of their religion/club and that too under the cover of NGO: THEY ARE INSTRUMENTAL IN BREAKING INDIA AND IT IS HIGH TIME MODI DISMANTLES AND MAKES THEM DEPART URGENTLY OR ELSE PEOPLE WILL GET REALLY FRUSTRATED IF BJP WAITS ONE MORE YEAR. PLEASE MODIJI, ACTION ONLY CAN BE USEFUL AND WORDS NOW HAVE NO USE: PEOPLE WANT LAW ABOLISHING THE MAJORITY OF THEM BY OINE ARTICLE OF LAW.

Not knowingly a goat followed a wolf and now that that brainwashed goat wants other goats to join him and plays all kinds of tricks to cheat those who won't follow him. This analogy applies also perfectly to the Indian who embraces Christianity and then invites his friends and family to join him. But, the Western wolf is laughing all the way to his bank now because once his coffers were empty as church is losing its lustre in the west but with conversions in INDIA and the ease with which they can fool the Hindus, they are too happy to reap money in millions and can only laugh at us thinking we are easily manipulated by simple techniques that will never work in any other country .

They now fill their empty coffers with Indian rupees ; How they make a livelihood out of lying ? they come here to CONVERT our people by implementing "JOSHUA project" that clearly states its objective is to plant a church in every Indian village that they identify based on the data of our postal pin code system...Thus they want to plant a church in every postal pin code area (it is written in the manifesto of this organisation" Joshua project") : let us say "no" to this dupery... LET our brothers and sisters who have already converted need not worry , they still can return to our ancestors' way of seeing God in the multiplicity of creation and not in only one Middle east authoritarian man born in a desert whose face was originally semi-black but painted as a white European with blue eyes to cheat the Europeans and the Americans first and now those duped men from the west want to dupe Indians ! That only reminds me of the story of a jackal who lost his tail and made others believe that he cut it off willingly because it was the fashion of the day. What is the biggest threat to INDIA?

Church infiltration in university and research institutions.

Why Mysore university approves "south Asian institute of advanced Christian studies course on "how to convert north Indians"! Why govt owned BHEL donates to south Asian institute of advanced Christian studies to teach "how to convert north Indians? »

http://www.saiacs.org/Research-NorthIndia.html

http://www.saiacs.org/Academics-Intro.html

http://fcraonline.nic.in/fc3_verify.aspx?RCN=0944 20397R&by=2011-2012

TWO EPISODES OF CHRISTIANITY WENT not so well reported, publicised and researched; Inquisition in GOA during Portuguese rule and anti-Hindu atrocities during French colonisation in PONDICHERY, my native place. IT is not that we lack historical evidence of that epoch; In, Pondicherry, a Tamil who worked under the French colonial leaders as an assistant.

 Mr Ranga Pillai had written a book under French rule that describes in a painstakingly detailed manner how Hindus were tortured and humiliated / SHIVA temple desacralized and linga and other deities destroyed and churches erected at that place by the FRENCH colonial masters of that time.

IF YOU EXPLORE THE DIARY OF ANANDA RANGA PILLAI, you will be shocked to read so many atrocities committed against SHIVA TEMPLES: please spread awareness (originally in French, somebody had translated in to English).

FORMULA 22)

Modern warfare is unleashed on enemy countries by buying their media in the name of globalisation and commercial purpose but working as TROJAN HORSES inside that country to make propaganda to attain western evangelist's Hindu soul harvesting objectives. HERE IS THE EXCERPT FROM A RESEARCH PAPER ON OWNERSHIP OF INDIAN MEDIA;

In 2001, India had 45,974 newspapers, including 5,364 daily newspapers published in over 100 languages. The largest number of newspapers were published in Hindi (20,589), followed by English (7,596), Marathi (2,943), Urdu (2,906), Bengali (2,741), Gujarati (2,215), Tamil (2,119), Kannada (1,816), Malayalam (1,505) and Telugu (1,289). The Hindi daily press has a circulation of over 23 million copies, followed by English with over 8 million copies.

There are several major publishing groups in India, the most prominent among them being the Times of India Group, the Indian Express Group, the Hindustan Times Group, The Hindu group, the Anandabazar Patrika Group, the Eenadu Group, the Malayalam Manorama Group, the Mathrubhumi group, the Sahara group, the Bhaskar group, and the Dainik Jagran group.

India has more than 40 domestic news agencies. The Express News Service, the Press Trust of India, and the United News of India are among the major news agencies. Let us see the ownership of different media agencies.

Do you know that NDTV, a popular TV news media is funded by GOSPELS of charity of SPAIN?

This media house developed a soft corner for PAKISTAN and it enjoyed support from Pakistan government and this explains why NDTV gained access to PAKISTAN market!

The CEO of this TV is PRANNOY ROY who is co-brother of PRAKASH KARAT, Secretary of Communist Party of India.

India Today which used to be the rare national weekly which supported BJP is now bought by NDTV!! Since then the tone has got a new colour with Hindu bashing as main focus.

CNN-IBN is a 100% Southern Baptist Church funded media house with its headquarters in the US. The Church allocates $ 800 million annually. The Indian head of this channel is RAJDEEP SARDESAI and his wife Sagarika GHOSH.

Times group list: Times Of India, Mumbai – Mirror, Nav-Bharth Times, Stardust, Femina, Vijaya Times, Vijaya Karnataka, Times now (24- hour news channel) and many more. Times Group is owned by Bennet & Coleman. "World Christian Council" own shares up to 80 percent and the rest is owned by the Italian Robertio Mindo who is a close relative of Sonia Gandhi, the leader of the opposition party congress (it is no more a full-fledged opposition party either since the last elections of 2019).

Star TV is run by the Australian Rupert MURDOCH who gets funding from ST PETERS PONTIFICAL CHURCH MELBOURNE.

Hindustan Times is owned by BIRLA GROUP but has embraced the Times Group since some time.

The Hindu is only Hindu in its name but it is 100% anti-Hindu and gets regular funding from JOSHUA society, BERNE, Switzerland.

Indian Express comprises of two groups: The Indian Express and new Indian Express. ACTS MINISTRIES, a Christian proselytization enterprise has stakes in this group.

Even the Statesman is controlled by the "breaking India" Communist Party of INDIA with Marxist ascendency.

Asian Age is linked with a Saudi Arabian company whose editor in chief is none other than MJ Akbar.

So, now you can see why the media is anti-Hindu because it is controlled by foreign CHRISITAN AND PROTESTANT CHURCHES whose obsession is to convert all 1 billion Hindus of INDIA TO CHRISTIANITY. Very nice, you see?

Not everything can be attributed to American CIA or any other external sources but also to our OWN mental attitude going after copying anything western without first asking the question : "how this alien technique of architecture, agriculture, horticulture, manufacturing , road and infrastructure building, which were the consequences of a different specific conditions , can be adapted to our specific geographical, topographical, geological, climatic local particularities so that we make the best choice for a sustainable and a pleasant environment ?"

IMPACT OF MACAULAY ON THE INDIAN COLLECTIVE PSYCHE

Here is an interesting quote from the speech by Lord Macaulay who said the following about India in 1835 in British Parliament:

I QUOTE Macaulay: «I have travelled across the length and breadth of India and I have not seen one person who is a beggar, who is a thief. Such wealth I have seen in this country, such high moral values, people of such calibre, that I do not think we would ever conquer this country, unless we break the very backbone of this nation, which is her spiritual and cultural heritage, and, therefore, I propose that we replace her old and ancient education system, her culture, for if the Indians think that all that is foreign and English is good and greater than their own, they will lose their self-esteem, their native self-culture and they will become what we want them, a truly dominated nation." End of quote.

The **English Education Act 1835** was a legislative Act proposed by the then Council of India; the act supported funding Indian education by favouring English language and depriving local vernacular languages from funds; the political will was thus translated in to legislative act so that INDIANS are educated in English and not in their native language.

This led eventually to English becoming one of the languages of India, rather than simply the native tongue of its foreign rulers.

Essential points to remember from the speech of Macaulay in the British parliament:

In discussions leading up to the Act THOMAS BABINGTON MACAULAY delivered his speech in which he expressed his desire to replace teaching Indian languages in schools with English language so that England can produce Indians who are externally Indians but think, speak, act like an Englishman.

Here I quote him : " <u>There was therefore a need to produce—by English-language higher education—"a class of persons, Indian in blood and colour, but English in taste, in opinions, in morals and in intellect" who could in their turn develop the tools to transmit Western learning in the vernacular languages of India.</u> End of quote.

He wanted to put a full stop to education in Sanskrit or Arabic language.

With English "Macaulay" system mingled with MISSIONARY education network, we are moulded since childhood in the same matrix as European children. So, MODI, the PRIME MINISTER OF INDIA, should dismantle slowly that type of education and replace with our unique vedic system of GURUKAL with so many qualities if at all one day the western came to know that system, the whole America would copy it (they are intelligent enough to know which is good from India and which is not and make quick and better choices. They have already adopted YOGA and Meditation in their daily or weekend routine). Now, when that time will come,

India would be weaker than the Americans in mastering their own inherited vedic knowledge.

When I speak of western imperialists, I speak of only those "bourgeoisie class" of the USA and the Europe instigating globalisation tailor made to their greed not those poor innocent silent masses of America or Europe. Those millions of Americans and Europeans are carefully denied vital information like whenever they give donations to a Christian Trust, it is mischievously used to destroy a traditional culture by planting and thrusting their churches and converting people by financial and other allurements and cunning "divide and rule" strategy. Thus, their donations are so badly used that they cause more suffering than that which the worst poverty can afflict them.

Bagavat Gita advises us not to do anything against the dharmic principle that is "swyadharma" (to know more about the unique concept of dharma , consult this link :

and being detached from the changing time and destiny of the external world and search for inner stability.

USA and EUROPE should reclaim their pagan roots more respectful of man and nature. Their original roots lie in "dharmic" culture.

Whatever money you spend, (that you could have spent for the welfare of the poor in your country) on spying and manipulating other countries because you want to rule over others, that money is not well spent but all your efforts and dollars to enslave others is useless and going to gutters and septic tank. Why? First, the answer to this question is in the above statement itself.

Whenever and whatever you do, if your action's motive or hidden goal or ulterior desire is not in accordance with the universal principle that is a sort of universal natural law of ethics or as Indians call so beautifully "DHARMA", then your action will sow "karmic seeds" that will boomerang to you. This law is the foundation of our survival on earth and in BAGAVAT GITA which is now a familiar text to Americans thanks to "Hare Rama Hare Krishna», it is well explained how and why we should abide by this natural law to attain true peace and joy without any superficial "painting" or "make-up"

Also, it is useless to run BIG organisations with taxpayers' money to waste time on inventing new conspiracies and cunning plans day and night on the following subject "How to topple governments and subvert societies?"

Instead, they should ask this one: "how to sow "good deeds" so that we as a society or country can reap "good benefits"?

Why ask others to know which is bad or good, ask your intuition that is the inner guidance from the divine that we call Shiva. (Moreover, our innate feeling or our natural adherence to this law is due to accumulative "punya" of all the "good karma" of our ancestors and I have to say that we are depleting that source of "punya" fastly and furiously.)

Moreover, when you are exposed by truth coming out in the media, you are like a thief caught red handed. when WIKILEAK leader MR ASSANGE made you tremble, then what is the use of big big organisations with tax money??? JUST dismantle them and proceed by dealing with others in a spirit of "equality" not thinking they are inferior to you.

I don't say abandon your army and military preparedness, I say only that obsession and addiction should not go to unacceptable levels of paranoia or greed or fear.

Oligarchs of the USA! you should change this imperialistic approach just for your own good and that of the silent majority of wise American middle-class people.

The "bourgeois class of the USA" (politicians' nexus with bankers and industrialists) should apply more ethical or dharmic methods and abandon cunning strategies to subvert Asia and Africa.

Then only can they reap fruits of peace and prosperity instead of crisis and chaos. BAGAVAT GITA says, "whatever you sow, so you will reap" every action will come back hit you more heavily than you think and more quickly. Then, why spend money uselessly on thinking tanks that produce only "intellectual smoke" from cerebral heating, so useless for humans? CIA should be slimmed and all fat taken so that a mean CIA concentrates on effective defence of their country inside America and on human well-being of the USA population without interfering constantly in countries like NIGERIA or NICARAGUA or TITI CACA. I only condemn excess not the normal functioning of CIA or other spying organisations for your national interests, the measure of which I leave to your own judgement. Judging from how they function in India, I can only advise them to adapt their strategies to the quality of the people and the society in a highly spiritual country like India in the perspective of dharma and proceed to accomplish their missions not just acting only with the principle "no matter what measures I take if at all

they yield results that I have fixed to myself "
mentality.

PART 2:

THIS FORMULA IS APPLIED TO THE WHOLE WORLD UNDER THE PRETEXT OF GLOBALISATION: IT 's OBJECTIVE AND EFFECT IS TO MAKE PEOPLE INDIFFERENT TO EACH OTHER AND LIVE IN INDIVIDUAL BODY PRISONS ALOOF FROM EACH OTHER.

MY DREAMS ABOUT A HARMONIOUS DEVELOPMENT

THAT DOES NEITHER STOP JOB CREATION NOR DESTROY OUR ENVIRONMENT.

We see the fruits of development in western world : first industrial revolution concentrates in few urban areas serial and massive units of standard production of consumer products then people move to those sites to fill the vacuum to contribute to that production, thus they tend to leave villages to live in urban areas, then all kinds of transport problems happen to remedy the first problem which was just caused by greed that made some capitalists forward industrial solutions in the first place, so step by step we are sucked by the vacuum of those greed motivated people who pump all human and natural resources to fulfil their greed; development without greed and in accordance with dharma can bloom and blossom ? And how it can happen? Can people be made to find joy and bliss in villages so that their exodus to dirty towns stop? CAN we imagine a development in a harmoniously covering all geographies without concentrating itself in few areas because of private initiative based on greed? CAN WE give more importance to small and medium companies and discourage big units except when they are justified by a social contribution that cannot be done by smaller units? Small is beautiful and can be also job creating, what is your take? Can we imagine a DEVELOPMENT taking care of ecology and sustaining earthly resources and also spreading in a multidirectional and harmonious way in contrast to concentration in some big urban cities? CAN WE not imagine a human size and more locally rooted development thus making colossal infrastructure unnecessary because of workplace/living place distance being minimized WHEN PRODUCTION UNIT pops up in small size but in big numbers not only in towns but also in villages? Should not government orient their policy to support that harmonious development WITH ZERO IMPACT ON OUR natural biological diversity? Can't we imagine like in FRANCE where the polluters should pay and other legislative measures to completely stop

Ganges and other rivers pollution by leather industries? India needs jobs in millions and anything that can put few robots to make millions of cars can only be damaging to her specificity AND HOW can we accommodate these two antagonistic forces? IN CHENNAI all Japanese and Americans have heavily invested but nothing (except Technicians controlling machines or workers doing a repetitive gesture from morning to evening) goes to create jobs for the size of India? By making villagers stay where they are, the need for cars will go down slowly. Infrastructure to help car capitalists will also become useless. When state bank of India face so much hurdles to open a branch in the USA why we give them easy access to our market? When they can come here and buy media and propagated anti India news, should government make amendments in fixing foreign shares in such a way they have no say what so ever or just made to quit India if they do not bring "new" technology? WHAT IS THE NEED for UNILEVER, PEPSI, COCA COLA, MC DONALD, MONSANTO, CARGIL, DOW CHEMICALS etc. in INDIA? Should we not make them quit India? They concentrate in them all greed that was the root pattern of the thought process of the Americans: what you are inside and how you think inside your mind come out in open daylight and is exposed before everyone in their actions and speeches. And their products and their food items. They epitomise greed in their products and goods and in their mega malls. We Indians should not get attracted by this "miroir aux allouettes" as they call in FRANCE and retain our "inner quality" as rose retains perfume, teck wood retains its hardness, water retains its purity.

Before I go "hors sujet" out of subject, here I am back with the concise formula that foolish politician's world over apply to make one another alien and aloof to each other:

Build big + 5 floor building everywhere knowing that all social specialists say it will only alienate people among themselves, making them egoists and individuals breaking apart all social feeling of belonging to one country.

Encourage greedy industrialists build big industries with the concept of concentrating 1000 people under one roof.

Create big distance between living place and working place by this concentration of industries in specific zones in and out urban areas.

Push people to take to the transportation system and middle-class people to use cars because of the distance thus created.

Encourage industries and discourage agriculture by all means making agriculture profitless business so that farmers flood urban cities.

Make everything to push this exodus to its maximum so that villages will be deserted by youths who crowd the already overcrowded cities in search of industrial or service-oriented jobs.

WHY IKEA entry in India will finish off the traditional wood craftsmanship skills of Indians?

It is always the western oligarchy who will benefit and get profits by opening IKEA, it is only a minority people belonging to a system composed of trio: bankers, majority shareholders of the industries and commerce of distribution and we? BUY AND BE QUIET. In the meanwhile, wood carpenters in millions are going to commit suicide professionally. The manufacturing quality is much stronger in traditional fashion than in IKEA fashion at the chain. These latter provide disposable furniture that breaks after a few years (pre-programmed wear) cause the exhaustion of our forests while in traditional dose the pace allowed the regrowth of cut trees. My own experience, when I compare the furniture that I used in my childhood (solid in teak or other traditional wood of India) and what I was forced to pay in FRANCE with unique industrial junk furniture offer, there is a big difference in quality and especially durability,

In India, an average family can access to traditional solid furniture in teak, (the cost in general allows it) and we in EUROPE cannot afford to buy the same traditional quality because it does not exist no more only industrial junk furniture . IKEA LOW QUALITY do it yourself (anti job creation system) industrial furniture.

Industrialisation is a by-product of greed and MNCs like IKEA will rush to India in a few years after exhausting CHINA

BECAUSE ONLY to the material world, they identified themselves, they yielded to the call of "greed" , so they wanted to subjugate other people to steal their wealth, 2) because they understood becoming rich is through industrialisation of production when they were exploiting INDIA, they established the same system that they perfected in their colonies, in their own countries of Europe and launched the "industrial revolution" 3) Because they wanted to sell you industrialised standardised food , they wanted to ensure its shelf life to support transportation and storage duration, 4) because of the greed to get richer as quickly as possible through IP and pro-western patent rules, they invented pesticides, fertilisers, GMO to grow your crops faster ignoring the risk to your health, they manipulated your crop genetically, they invented fridges, and big trucks; because they wanted a servile consumer who thinks as closely as they, they wanted to boost Christianity as a TOOL to standardize the THINKING PATTERN OF INDIANS.

It seems certain now that Indians are losing their culture and values due to westernization? It seems as if Indians value everything from the west more than their own creation. Is modernization ruining India? Has western ideology highly influenced our lifestyle?

When you Know that every thought has some result in your body, you can conclude that to be healthy it is better to have positive thoughts; But what about the thought of sex? BECAUSE, between sex performed in dharmic conditions with you husband or wife and that performed outside the dharmic fence, your bio-memory sees the difference and make you healthy when it is performed in a dharmic way but causes many nervous troubles (including sex-related troubles) when it detects that you have crossed the lines. YOU CAN NOT CHEAT YOUR BIO MEMORY WHICH SENDS SIGNALS TO YOUR MIND OF YOUR INNER FEELINGS THAT YOU MAY HIDE TO OTHERS OR TO YOURSELF; Your pleasure from a adharmic bond is really not worth the risk and the sense of adventure that can spring in you can only be a bad counselor and a bad adviser. This voice that incites you to go astray is that of your enemy who does not care for your health. And how you get ideas of such adharmic attractions? through your eyes. Eyes are the most cunning and betraying enemy. It can kill you slowly by letting inside your inner space images of lust; Beware of the negative power of this eyes which may seem innocent little things. So, what you give to the eyes will rule you and will become your master. Internet needs government intervention so that laws and special force track pornographic content; India before the arrival of Internet and India as it is now are not the same; It is the one drop of poison which makes the whole food of Indian culture poisonous and uneatable ready to be dumped as garbage; THE WESTERN CULTURE is not automatically a solution for India; We should not copy them because they have thousands of problems that you do not have yet completely but you will have them very quickly ..... Now, imitating in the foolish way they treat their eyes with carelessness by feeding those predators with porno images will only destroy Bharat culture and dump everything you represent to the garbage!

WHY INDIANS SHOULD GO TO THEIR VEDIC EDUCATION SYSTEM?

The present situation is but the result of a path that you or your forefathers chose many years or millennia before : when your forefather lived under British, he had to adapt himself to the social conditions of that epoch so he replaced all the valuable traditions with that of the prevailing ones and slowly he left behind him the "gurukulam" education and had to choose a "compartmentalized and specialized way of learning one discipline at a time with no understanding of the global and universal bird's eye-view of all subjects and their interconnection that existed in our school system of "gurukulam".

Example : the concept of "prakriti" as an aspect of God , Purusha is that it is just an outcome of the divine leela and it is all pervaded by the universal spiritual Paramatma that while living in everyone can also live outside us and that this connection teaches us that the 5 elements (air, earth, ether, fire , water), the basic building blocks of the universe, are also inside our body in "vatta, pitta, kapha" and "the corresponding principles "sattvikam, rajas and tamash" the first related to virtue, the second to the pursuit of "parkriti or material's manifestations from the infinite combinations of the five elements " that man transform in to other objects , be it a "industrialized transformed matter like a car or a shoe or a house etc" Thus having understood that matter's million forms are derived only from the different combinations of the 5 elements, we can understand the global holistic knowledge of everything and their inter-dependency. Now, the western world whom we followed blindly had understood and de-learning their own stuff and re-learning (example: patenting cunningly our Ayurvedic herbs, copying yoga, meditation etc and re-labelling it under different names etc) what our forefathers taught to us once. So, now when the western people say" everything is connected at quantic level" we say "yes, amen" and embrace them.

We should understand that we were following like blind persons someone who was equally blind AND also GRAVELY handicapped. While rejecting the enlightening masters of our country, we throw to the dustbin our own knowledge whose truth is now revealed one by one by the science?

BECAUSE of many factors: colonization that created a situation wherein being Indian was perceived as "uncivilized" and so we were taught to think low of ourselves and feel ashamed of ourselves because we accepted without any "critical study and analysis" whatever we were spoon fed by the BRITISH and their Indian sepoys. This British social, economic, educational, fake electoral "democracy" system (ours was based on" panchayat" localized system) gave us "inferiority complex" from which we are still suffering. Indian education is still based on English-medium education even after 50 years after independence. (so, are we really free?). We may be proud Indians but we are building under tropics housed adapted to cold countries ! we bring up our children with western "desire" and are unable to extirpate them from the grips of "tight pants" "short thigh showing shorts" "high heels" and "winter coats" more adapted to a freezing climate of Europe than ours !

Here is the list of American secret groups and their paid local agents: NGOS, Human Rights org, GREEN REVOLUTION sepoy SAMINATHAN, globalization man coolie MANMOHAN SINGH, missionaries from VATICAN and the USA who indulge in geographical and cultural rape of India, media cum cinema actors recruited to proselytise innocent folks by taking names like James , George etc with their Hindu names ..THE FORD FOUNDATION AND NOW CARNEGIE ENDOWMENT AND thousand other trusts (even among them a foundation for our enviable "mustard"), Some intellectual NOBEL and other prize snatchers, now you should add , sadly , judges who want to ban jallikattu and PETA {they distribute insemination of European cattle and contribute to the complete extermination of Indian cows which give more healthier milk than European cows }. why do they do all this? First , Americans in their majority are exploited and duped by 1% of their population and this minority tries to lay hands on wherever they suspect a source of wealth and I told him perhaps that the Americans came from Europe where absence of sun made crop, fruits and vegetable grow only on certain terrains so they knew what it is to live on a survival mode eating pigs and wearing animal skins and searching to escape the snow cold climate by all means and each and every second and so their bio-memory made them aware of the quality of land and India's quality of land with its waterways and sunrays on 365 days a year made it the most potentially rich country on the planet ; besides such a potentially rich country is also the one with an important cultural and religious heritage of an exceptionally high intellectual standard that can beat the hell out of their Bible; So, controlling such a country ensures the American oligarchy keep money from India flow to their pockets maintaining their power intact in their own native country too and making the majority of masses of the USA their slaves ... I added the story of an Indian who invented plastic road and as soon as he did so, somebody from the USA bought it as quickly as bullet escaping the barrel of a gun. So, they know to respect inventions in a condensed form crystallised for eternity in the non-sense concept of "brevet" and "patent" and exploit whoever has that creative power to patent and control their creation. This minority spends his 80 years or so they live on this planet to propagate this non-sense of the mind-set of not sharing anything with anybody even with their mother! In one word, they want to control Indians for power, money because their mentality is based on superficial greed and not on essential need.

INDIAN FARMERS VERSUS FOREIGHN MULTI-NATIONAL GMO COMPANIES

Some few years back, the Indian government banned salt without iodine. Those who have no machines to manufacture this salt will lose their daily bread in favour of the western company's Indian subsidiary: Hindustan lever. (What is the word "Hindustan" doing in this foreign company?) We know that the compulsory manufacture of iodised salt cannot be for health reasons ALONE. We know that a surfeit of iodine is harmful. We know that iodised salt is expensive because iodine must be imported; we know that the plastic bagging process necessary to the preservation of the iodine content is polluting on a massive scale; we know that the mandatory policy is ruining small workers; we know that the policy is driven by the greed of multinational corporations and organizations; we know that industrial iodisation is inefficient; that the lack of iodine is due to fertilizers in the soil; that the way Indians cook means that iodine evaporates during the cooking process, rendering iodisation pointless. We know that banning un-iodised salt when tobacco and alcohol are freely available is undemocratic. The human race has survived for millions of years without using iodised salt. What is the urgent need to ban the poor man's salt if not to please a white man who has deep pockets and whose sole thought is to get richer and richer even at the cost of making Indian farmers poorer and poorer?

The supermarket chains, including Wal- mart and Carrefour, are not just exporting to other nations; they are also taking over food retailing in the poorer countries. Small traditional workers are unable to manufacture standardized products for the sake of large supermarkets. So, they are thrown out of business. Larger and larger farms, that have the ability to invest and work with the big MNCs, are driving poor farmers in Central American countries out of even the domestic market. Local growers are now competing against super-efficient and often subsidized mass producers. We can compare this situation to a battlefield where you have, on one side, a well-organised and well-equipped army and the on other side, a bunch of barehanded soldiers. Before the economic clout of Wal-Mart what can a poor Indian supplier can do? No match.

Wal- mart is spending huge amount of money to play lobbyer and participate in campaign funds, mostly for Republican candidates in the US. Even a few years ago, Wal-Mart spent next to nothing on lobbying to influence US-China trade negotiation in its favour. It succeeded to give a push to its Asian expansion plans. Wal-Mart is starting even to put its stamp on regulations.

People elect MLAs and MPs so that they will make better laws to help them to live a better life. But, if companies and their Trojan horse like IMF AND WORLD BANK influence Indian lawmakers to suit their needs where is Democracy? ???Politicians are elected to serve people's interests not to execute the diktat of the MNC's like slaves working to please their masters. Why those proxy arms of the US and Europe "the world bank" or "IMF make so much hype about free trade, being an important trait of democracy, before giving loans to poor countries?" IT'S DEMOCRACY BY THE MNC FOR THE MNC AND OF THE MNC!!!

Only the big can serve the big; the small has to die. And global companies will wipe out our local distinctions and make India a euro-American colony.

The failure of BTCOTTON seed sold by the American company MONSANTO

BT COTTON never yielded the publicised results!

This is the main reason for our farmers' suicide. Why the Indian authority, without any discussion, has accepted the Monsanto Company's test results???? Why Indian government has given license to BTCOTTON seed of this American MNC to be sold to poor farmers without testing its real worthiness by an independent lab? Are our farmers' lands a testing lab for those companies? Should our farmer bear the financial risk of those companies' product failure? The result is farmers had not only lost their harvests but also their lives. Recently, Monsanto tested gm food on rats that developed physical anomalies. Environmentalists and food security activists in India are alarmed at the result of the secret test conducted by Monsanto on rats with GM corn diets. Those rats developed blood and organ abnormalities. Do our government want Indian consumers to bleed in their beds and die a foolish death like those rats? Indian officials who are letting Monsanto 's seeds and goods sold in India should think that their children have to face the same health problem like any Indian consumer. WE SHOULD BAN UNSCRUPULOUS MNC's IN INDIA. Our politicians should not try to please powerful western lobbies but elaborate a new policy to circumvent this binding unscrupulous world trade policies where western negotiators are succeeding to slowly gain complete access to Indian market while keeping their market closed for our exporters by subsidising their farmers and their non-performing companies. Our people are closing their factories and shops and selling their agricultural assets to let foreign capital take possession of them. Is this India our forefathers wanted when they liberated India from the clutches of the British? What will happen if this situation gains ground? More and more Indians will go to the US and European countries in search of jobs. So, if the western power tries to wipe our entrepreneurship, it will only displace the crisis to their country. Every action has an equivalent and opposite reaction. Imperialist powers can never escape this law of karma.

The western world is obsessed with what they see in the external world while Indians turn their attention inwards so that they can first understand the functioning of their own mind before understanding that of others.

 A narcissist West is unable to see its own mistakes because the veil of ego blinds its eyes.

Take for example a man whose eyes are blocked by an invisible glass in which his only personal point of view reflects.

An ego is a reflection of oneself in one's mind 's mirror.

Such a suffering person is unable to see and admit his own mistakes.

Not surprisingly, the man who has this opaque glass is handicapped almost intellectually and is unable to exploit his full potential and creativity, thus his mind fixes his own limitations. when some third person sees what he himself cannot see, he will reject the third man's point of view!

Because the cat has closed its eyes, it thinks the whole world has darkened.

When someone reacts instantly to safeguard his pride, he is somewhere afraid that someone may criticise him and this shows his lack of courage to see himself as he is with his qualities and defects.

This man can only tolerate praises and he will discard even positive and useful criticism. How to progress if one is blocked by one own limitation????

Take for example the overconfident attitude of the BRITISH who seemed to have painted the so called "caste" in a colour that was not akin to reality:

How the BRITISH throw lot of mud over the age-old concept of division of labour according to one's innate capacity or propension by calling them as "caste system"? This word "caste" is derived from a Portuguese word "casta".

IF WE ACCEPT every human being should follow his swadharma and among human beings nobody is superior nor inferior, we can weed out some defects of the so called Portuguese "casta" system then we can transform it as an equivalent of a "lions club" or "economic club" where actors of a certain category find moral or financial support and can act as a repository of 1000 year conservation of knowledge without diluting it. There is no difference between LION OR ROTARY CLUB and our economic club ; Imagine a big mansion with a garden to be restored ; there should be architects to redesign it , some carpenters to equip it with new furniture, some engineers to restructure its broken structures , some workers to carry our cement work and brick laying and some to clean the garden and recycle the waste so there is a "national" project restoring a whole nation so Indians imagined, some 5000 years ago , a best system to share work among the capacity of each one of us and to make it efficient than a diploma from a university, they imagined a father son transmission of secrets incorporated to their profession equivalent to American "patent " so this was a knowledge conservation for centuries among members of a club " but what BRITISH made out of it made us shudder as if this is a system that cannot be reformed or receive some legal arrangements ! THAT SHOULD CHANGE we should just use it as an economic model that preserves jobs, knowledge keeping in mind ours is a "human relationship based " society not a "greed based "one.

INDIAN PERCEPTION OF THE INTERCOONNECTED NATURE OF ALL LIVING BEINGS INCLUDING PLANTS AND ANIMALS HELPED THEM TO GET A HOLISTIC VIEW OF THE UNIVERSE.

WE do not view earth as exploitable ONLY but our nourishing mother; the western people, on the contrary, see the earth with the same greed as a lion sees a prey. We don't fix rate to the speed with winch we drink the milk of our mother earth as GROWTH RATE

whatever the GDP or the rate of growth, these are western indicators to define the speed with which they exploited the earth of the colonised lands, if it is respectful of ecology, sustainable production, then ok; if not, what use of such development?

The rate of speed with which we grow may be interesting and healthy only if this rate indicates a "ethical quality" of our production such as organic food, sustainably managed forest wood, natural energy, derived from the sun, the wind instead of pumping from the limited and polluting fossil resources.

For a few centuries, the world has imposed on India communism, then capitalism, then globalization and now all these ideas of an ideal system of world economy collapsed and did not survive ... while the system that India has known for millennia is based on a localized economic model adsorbing the local workforce, using the micro-capital of the environment adapted for a production calibrated exactly to the volumes of local needs avoiding the necessity to spend on refrigeration equipment or in the use of chemical preservatives to prolong artificially shell life of products (causing cancer in human beings) ; because local production is transported faster to local consumers ensuring maximum freshness quality, we preserve health of consumers. This autonomous system that worked at the local level was based on human relations and not on greed. HINDUSTAN SHOULD OFFER THIS MODEL TO THE WORLD, A 5000 YEAR TIME TESTED MODEL

India should perfect this localised autonomous self-sufficient ECONOMIC SYSTEM where capital, workforce, production and distribution are localised and this system was relation based and not greed based; HINDUSTAN SHOULD OFFER THIS MODEL TO THE WORLD A 5000 + YEAR TIMES TESTED MODEL.

WESTERN OLIGARCHY wanted to impose imperialistic ideas for western capturing of world resources for 1% and the remaining should act as salary getting mass but that system will not encourage (because money is within the hands of 1%) entrepreneurship of the mass and transform them as modern salves , this system is not at all adapted to a heavily populated job starved country like India where micro companies should prop up every corner of the street to absorb youths offering their intellect and working capacity for the production and distribution world .

When you are obsessed with individual domination of the material world and exploit people to get richer than ideas to gather massive money through public participation is not a surprise!

So, the west invented "stock exchange" where companies' value was determined by buying and selling (demand and offer) of shares which is not a faithful reflection of the reality but a subjective impression of the public on a company's strength to grow.

The idea of this kind of channel for gathering money from everyone on the street can come only from a greed-based mind that of a western mind.

This accumulation of money and transfer to one entity or one man will only create monsters that can rival with governments as it is already the case. We see huge MNCs having an annual turnover equivalent to government budget of a third world country!

The root cause is here in this ferocious unlimited desire to grow grasp all resources for one person.

Another reform could be the disassociation of the stock exchange playing with a company value as if it is a game for children!

Can we separate the valuation of a company from the grip of the unstable stock exchange system and guarantee a minimum stability for those who own that company?

The system of collective ownership of a company need shares from you and me. But why that share 's value is abandoned to fluctuation of demand and offer of a market? Can't we work out a new system where the Bank justifies the amount of gold it stocks as notes and where the share 's values is equivalent to the balance sheet 's loss or profit at any given time? Is it possible to offer an alternative system for this fluctuating fake system of fixing values of a company for which employees work and die? Can we imagine a ceiling say 25% of the total investment needed to be from stock exchange and the rest from other internal sources that is from the funds from the working capital that the French call "fonds de roulement"?

Who is RAJIV MALHOTRA?

Rajiv Malhotra is an Indian of American nationality had written many books on India's myriad of social problems stemming from outside of India; He made INDIANS become conscious of their pathetic situation because of western interventions to brainwash them so that they may fit in to their agenda.

His books «breaking India" or "being different" are pathbreaking, for they inspired all INDIANS to think by themselves and see the world through their own lens instead of that borrowed from the west. I would recommend you to read his books so that you can understand the many challenges thrown at India and how can we tackle them, the first step being seeing them and identifying their source. So, Rajiv MALHOTRA's books can be an eye-opener AND EDUCATE YOUTHS OF INDIA ABOUT THEIR TRADITIONAL KNOWLEDGE SYSTEM.

CONCLUSION: THE DESSERT

Colonial massive impact on Indian's mindset cannot be got rid of in a few decades ..People of India were so much conditioned by the colonial education which is still vigorously moulding the minds of Indians, their problems appear unsolvable because Indians failed to understand themselves in their own language, on their own terms and see things through their own lens. We can learn from the West. We can emulate aspects of their well-functioning systems of local government and law and mingle it with dharma (or the basic principle based on which the entire universe functions, to create a better world). But even to learn from others we must study them from our own experience based on accumulated knowledge of many millennia. But how can we do that when India's entire academic social disciplines exist on borrowed terms and borrowed theories under heavy colonial influence of many centuries? how can we do that when we are heavily formatted our mindset and social collective codes of behaviour from alien culture that was meant for enhancing western powers commercial gains to fit perfectly in to their agenda and aligned to their tunes ?

Fear binds western societies with its corollary "policing and law-making". Fear binds Western societies while "free will from a dharma-abiding mind makes an Indian obey social codes without heavy policing as in the western world.

DHARMA had always been the foundation, the structure and the cement of our Bharat permeating each thought and act of our people where people respect social norms out of their free will and deep respect for the "Atman" inside more than appeal to their primitive instincts of fear and obedience which are two faces of the same coin.. INDIA is driven by Dharma consciousness and with a "name sake" policing and law-making, we have less crime rate than in the fear-based Europe or the USA.

Yes, Indians can rightly feel being one of the luckiest people on earth of having inherited such huge Vedic literature!

We are the luckiest on the planet to have inherited without asking anything a treasure that is refused to all others who live outside BHARAT. Why me? Am I so dear to you O! GOD! that you bestowed upon me this wonderful treasure? Let us share with the whole world this wonderful gift so extraordinary that you should have done many "punyas" during thousands of your past lives to deserve this gift of the Lord. It may seem so easy to be a Hindu that we may even take it for granted; but ask a western Hindu's frustration not being in your shoes because he could guess the beauty just seeing the surface and cannot have enough time and possibility to deepen his mastership over this elusive tradition and culture which seems so normal to you. Indeed, lucky was I of having the possibility to have listened to the recitation of the mantras when I was a child and going to bed having read the stories and epics of our heritage. Lucky was I to have heard thousands of stories that made my imagination fly to many unknown lokas or islands crossing the seven seas which would not been possible if I were born in any other nation than Bharat. Lucky was I when being an adolescent, I could see the beauty of the saree fluttering in the breeze and the incense making my senses ablaze. Lucky was I was when being an adult, I could find real a woman and not woman frustrated not being a man. Lucky of having known the feeling connection between members of the same family, the same society and the same country through an invisible bondage they call "values" but so indispensable to the foundation and the structure of the building "BHARAT".

For all these reasons, a world based on "universal ethics of dharma" can alone create a world in which mankind will enjoy a durable peace and prosperity.

Please visit my blog where I elaborated on the subject of this book. Here is its link:

https://panindiahindu.wordpress.com/